Hi, Neighbor!

Projects and Activities About Our Community

Written by Denise Bieniek

Illustrated by Laura Ferraro

10   9   8   7   6   5   4   3

This edition published in 2003.

Troll Early Learning Activities

Troll Early Learning Activities is a classroom-tested series designed to provide time-pressured teachers with a wide range of theme-related projects and activities to enhance lesson plans and enrich the curriculum. Each book focuses on a different area of early childhood learning, from math and writing to art and science. Using a wide range of activities, each title in this series is chockful of innovative ideas, handy reproducible pages, puzzles and games, classroom projects, suggestions for bulletin boards and learning centers, and much more.

With highly interactive student projects and teacher suggestions that make learning fun, Troll Early Learning Activities is an invaluable classroom resource you'll turn to again and again. We hope you will enjoy using the worksheets and activities presented in these books. And we know your students will benefit from the dynamic, creative learning environment you have created!

Titles in this series:

Animal Friends: Projects and Activities for Grades K-3

Circle Time Fun: Projects and Activities for Grades Pre-K-2

Classroom Decorations: Ideas for a Creative Classroom

Early Literacy Skills: Projects and Activities for Grades K-3

Helping Hands: Small Motor Skills Projects and Activities

Hi, Neighbor! Projects and Activities About Our Community

Number Skills: Math Projects and Activities for Grades K-3

People of the World: Multicultural Projects and Activities

Our World: Science Projects and Activities for Grades K-3

Seasons and Holidays: Celebrations All Year Long

Story Time: Skill-Building Projects and Activities for Grades K-3

Time, Money, Measurement: Projects and Activities Across the Curriculum

---

Metric Conversion Chart

1 inch = 2.54 cm	1 foot = .305 m	1 yard = .914 m
1 mile = 1.61 km	1 fluid ounce = 29.573 ml	1 cup = .24 l
1 pint = .473 l	1 teaspoon = 4.93 ml	1 tablespoon = 14.78 ml

Contents

Community Workers

Teacher for the Day 5

Parental Show and Tell 6

Carpenter Costume 7

Carpenter Costume Patterns 8-10

Jobs Jumble Flip Book 11-13

Best Books About Jobs 14

Shoe Patterns 15-16

Are You Ready to Order? 17-18

Reporter for a Day 19

Tools of the Trade 20

Kid Chefs 21

Applesauce Recipe..22

Production Problems..23

Communities Near and Far

Model Neighborhood..24

List of Errands File Folder Game......................25-28

Best Books About Communities 29

Sign Language 30

Take the Train 31

Neighborhood Numbers 32-33

At the Park 34

Supermarket ABCs 35

Shapes in Architecture..36

Transportation Concentration Game 37-39

Logic Boxes..40

Our Community Game 41

Community Field Trips..42

Classroom Government 43

Stone Soup 44

Stone Soup Puppets 45-46

Worldwide Travelers...47

Home and Family Life

What a Family Means..48

Dream House 49

"Time for Play" Mobile 50

Baby Talk 51

Fire Safety Bulletin Board 52

Safety First Bulletin Board 53

The World Around Us

Milk Carton Bird Feeder...................54

Recycling Rights and Wrongs 55

Environmental Word Search.................56

Our Weather 57

Animal Families..........................58

The Mitten 59

The Mitten Flannel Board 60-61

Community Service Award 62-63

Answers 64

Teacher for the Day

1. Brainstorm with the class about the job of a teacher. Do they think it is easy or hard? What do they think teachers do to prepare for class? How much schooling do they estimate it takes to become a teacher? Ask if anyone would like to try being a teacher.

2. Give each volunteer a slip of paper on which to write the subject he or she would like to teach. Before assigning each student a time slot, ask him or her to submit a lesson plan.

3. When a lesson is approved, assign time slots of 10 to 20 minutes per student (depending on lesson plan and ability level). Remind each child that you will be acting as a student and that he or she will be responsible (within reason) for providing an exciting lesson and for making sure each student knows what his or her role is if the lesson plan calls for the class to be divided into groups.

4. After all the volunteers have had a turn teaching, make an experience chart about their perceptions. Do they still have the same ideas and thoughts as before, or have some of their opinions changed?

5. As a follow-up activity, ask each student to interview a favorite teacher. Tell each child to think of four questions to ask the selected teacher. Help students set up appointments for their interviews. Encourage children to share with the class their questions and the answers the teachers gave.

Teacher for the Day	
Lisa	Math
Ryan	Spelling
Mike	Arts + Crafts
Karen	Science
Ann	Language Arts
Tricia	Social Studies
Rob	Penmanship

Miss Lisa: Math

$4 \times 1 = 4$

$4 \times 2 =$

Parental Show and Tell

1. Ask the class to design invitations asking parents to come to the classroom to talk about their careers (at home and out of the home), hobbies, and community activities.

2. Survey the parents to discover if any have talents for activities that could be done in the classroom, such as cooking, music, language, or art. Stagger the talks so that no more than two are scheduled per day.

3. Before each parent talks or performs, ask his or her child to introduce the parent to the class.

4. Tape the sessions and put the tapes in the listening center. If possible, take photographs to use to make a class book for each talk. Ask each student to write or dictate a comment about his or her parent for the book. Place each book with its tape in the listening center so students can visualize the experience while hearing each parent speak.

5. After students have enjoyed hearing the tapes and looking at the books, present each parent with his or her book as a reminder of the visit.

Carpenter Costume

Materials:

- crayons or markers
- scissors
- oaktag
- glue
- safety pins or tape

Directions:

1. Reproduce the tools and tool belt on pages 8–10 once for each student. Color the patterns, mount them on oaktag, and cut them out. Cut along the dash lines on the tool belt to make slits.

2. To make the measuring tape, glue the overlapping ends of each piece to form one long tape, as shown.

3. Mount the tools on oaktag and cut them out again. Have each child place them in the appropriate tool belt "pockets."

4. Use a safety pin or tape to attach the tool belt to each student's shirt or to the belt loops of his or her pants.

5. Teach the class the following song and movements to perform while wearing their carpenter costume.

I Am a Crafty Carpenter
(to the tune of "I Am a Fine Musician")

I am a crafty carpenter.
I build things every day.
And I can hammer this nail
In a special way.
Bang, bang, bang, bang, bang, bang, bang, bang.
(students take out hammer and pretend to hammer in a nail)

I am a crafty carpenter.
I build things every day.
And I can fix this loose screw
In a special way.
Turn, turn, turn, turn, turn, turn, turn, turn.
(students take out screwdriver and pretend to turn in a screw)

I am a crafty carpenter.
I build things every day.
And I can saw this piece of wood
In a special way.
Push, pull, push, pull, push, pull, push, pull.
(students pretend to saw a piece of wood)

I am a crafty carpenter.
I build things every day.
And I can measure anything
In a special way.
One, two, three, four, five, six, seven, eight.
(students pull out measuring tape and pretend to measure)

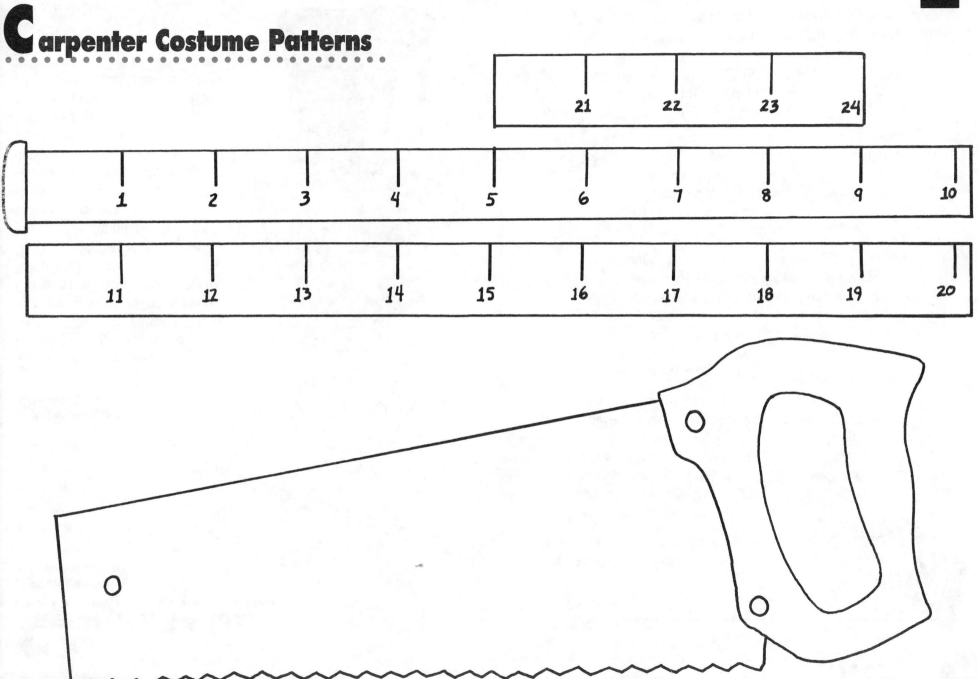

Carpenter Costume Patterns

21   22   23   24

1   2   3   4   5   6   7   8   9   10

11   12   13   14   15   16   17   18   19   20

Carpenter Costume Patterns

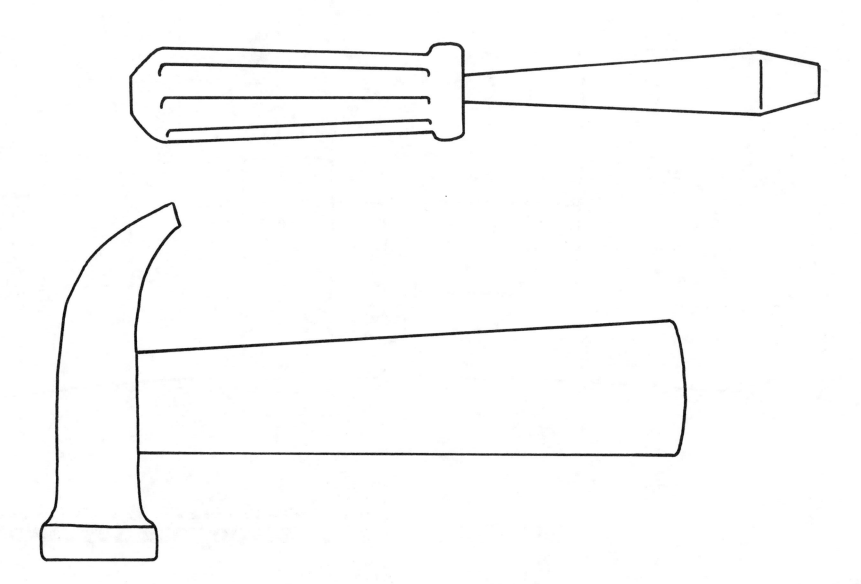

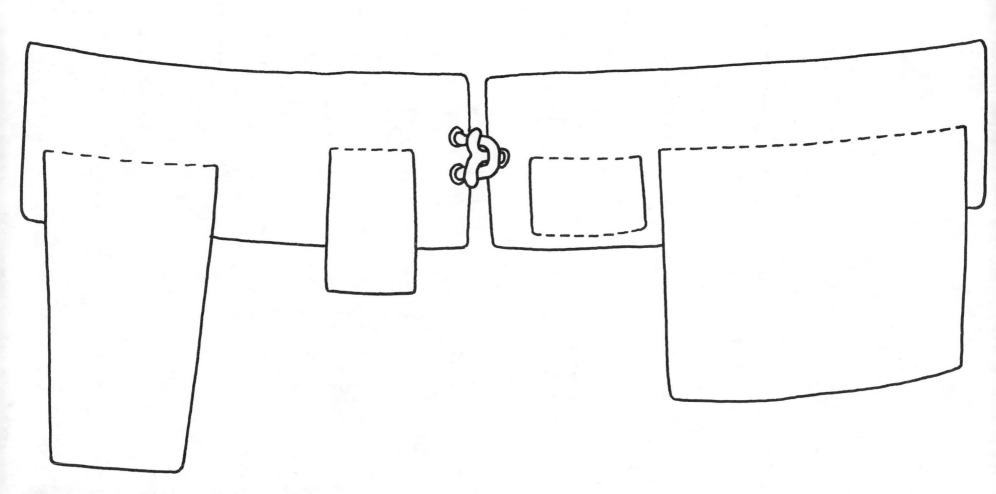

Carpenter Costume Patterns

Jobs Jumble Flip Book

Materials:

- crayons or markers
- scissors
- construction paper
- glue
- stapler

Directions:

1. Cut enough sheets of construction paper in half widthwise to allow 10 half-sheets per child.

2. Reproduce the job pictures on pages 12 and 13 once for each child. Have students color the pictures, cut them out, and glue them to half-sheets of construction paper.

3. Have the students use the remaining two half-sheets for the cover and back pages of the books. Encourage students to design titles and cover pictures for the books.

4. Place the job pictures for each book in a pile, putting the back page on the bottom of the pile and the cover on top. Staple along the left edge, as shown.

5. On each job page, cut along the dash line to the binding.

6. To mix and match jobs, have students flip the top half of a page, leaving the bottom half as is. Or students may wish to flip through the bottom half of the book and leave the top half in place.

7. Have students see how many different combinations they can create!

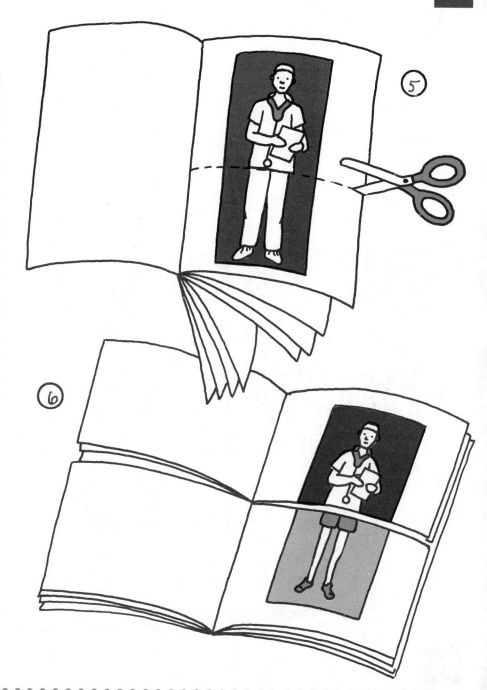

Jobs Jumble Flip Book

Jobs Jumble Flip Book

Best Books About Jobs

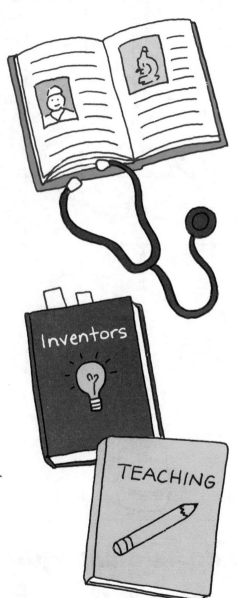

Read some or all of the following books to the class during a study unit about careers and community workers. Place the books in the class library or reading center for students to look at during free time.

Animal Doctor by Betsy Imershein (Messner, 1988)

Girls Can Be Anything by Norma Klein (Dutton, 1975)

How to Be an Inventor by Harvey Weiss (HarperCollins, 1980)

I Can Be a Teacher by Beatrice Beckman (Childrens Press, 1985)

My Father's Luncheonette by Melanie Hope Greenberg (Dutton, 1991)

People Who Make a Difference by Brent Ashabranner (Dutton, 1989)

What's It Like to Be an Airline Pilot by Judith Bauer (Troll, 1990)

What's It Like to Be an Astronaut by Susan Poskanzer (Troll, 1990)

What's It Like to Be a Chef by Susan Poskanzer (Troll, 1990)

What's It Like to Be a Doctor by Judith Bauer (Troll, 1990)

What's It Like to Be a Forest Ranger by Michael J. Pellowski (Troll, 1989)

When We Grow Up by Anne Rockwell (Dutton, 1981)

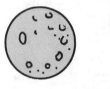

Shoe Patterns

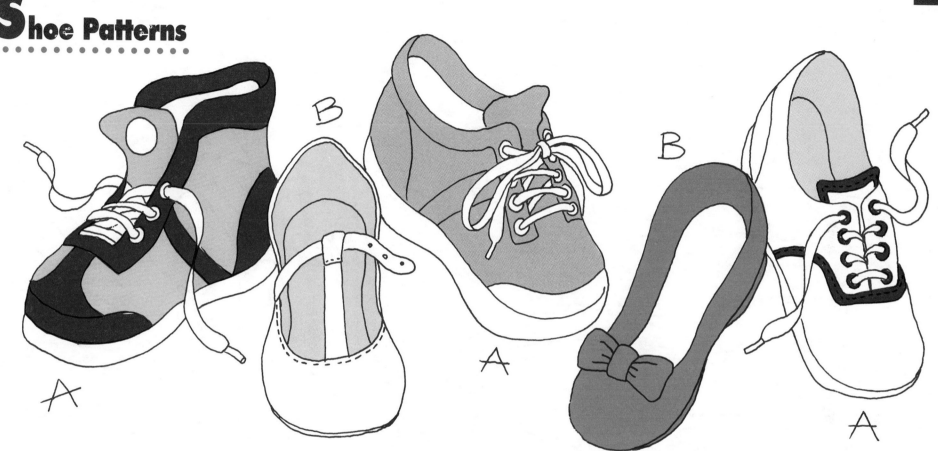

1. Ask the class if anyone knows what a cobbler is. Explain the importance of shoe making, and discuss the different types of shoes and the different sizes. Point out the styles for children and those for adults. Borrow a foot measure and measure the children's feet. Have the students practice putting on shoes with a shoe horn.

2. Try to find books that show shoe styles through the years and those of different countries. Show the class styles that they know and those that are particularly useful for a specific climate or place (such as sandals, rubber boots, and hiking boots).

3. Ask each child to remove one shoe. Collect the shoes and ask volunteers to try to create patterns with them. Some suggestions: AB AB AB (sneaker, party shoe; sneaker, party shoe), AAB AAB AAB (sandal, sandal, boot; sandal, sandal, boot), ABC ABC ABC (laces, Velcro, buckle; laces, Velcro, buckle), and so on.

4. After all the volunteers have taken a turn creating a pattern, reproduce the shoe pictures on page 16 several times for each student. Have children color the pictures and cut them out.

5. Tell students to work in groups of four or five students each. Ask children to create a shoe pattern using as many of the shoes they have as possible.

6. When each group is satisfied with its pattern, ask children to glue the shoes onto a long strip of butcher paper. Have the other students try to guess what pattern has been created.

Shoe Patterns

Are You Ready to Order?

Materials:

- crayons or markers
- scissors
- oaktag
- construction paper
- glue
- clipboard
- paper
- apron
- play money (optional)

Directions:

1. Reproduce the money patterns on page 18 ten times or more. Color the money, mount it on oaktag, and cut it out.

2. Divide the class into groups of four or five. Have each group design a menu for a restaurant of its own. Tell children to decide what type of eating establishment their menu will be for, what kinds of food to put on the menu, and what prices they will ask. Have them fold a piece of construction paper widthwise for the menu, and write in the foods and prices they have decided on. Put several sheets of paper headed "check" on the clipboard.

3. Choose one student from each group to be the server. He or she wears the apron and holds the clipboard. The rest of the group will be the customers. Both the server and the customers should be supplied with play money.

4. Have the customers sit at a table and look through the menu for something to order. They may order full meals or just a snack. Ask the server to write up the order and put the price of each item next to it.

5. Tell the customers to decide whether they wish to pay separately or together. After the server has added up the cost of the order(s), customers must pay, using play money. The server should make change as necessary.

6. Switch roles in order to give everyone a chance to be the server. For younger children, you may wish to have two children serve together and work as a team. For older children, try adding tax and a tip to each bill.

Are You Ready to Order?

Reporter for a Day

Now you can give the real scoop! Imagine that you're writing an article to go along with the picture below for your local newspaper. Remember to include details in your story. And don't forget the six important questions you need to answer—who, what, where, why, when, and how. Give your story a catchy title.

_____

_____

_____

_____

_____

_____

_____

_____

_____

_____

_____

Tools of the Trade

Different community workers use different tools. Draw a line to connect each tool to the community worker who needs it.

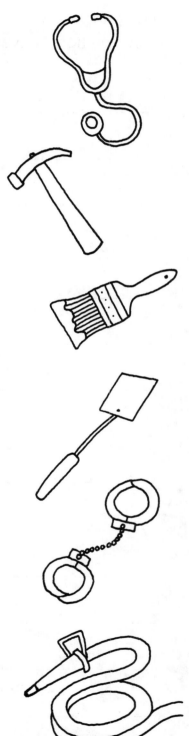

Kid Chefs

1. Invite a chef or baker to the class to give a simple demonstration. Some procedures that may interest the class are cutting food with knives, rolling dough, making a pizza, or making chocolates.

2. After the demonstration, encourage students to ask the visitor questions, such as:

> When did you decide to become a chef?
> What kind of training did you have?
> What kinds of foods do you like to cook?
> What is your favorite food to eat?
> Do you work in a restaurant?
>   If not, where do you work?
> What kinds of tools do you use?

3. Help each student make the apron below to wear when making the recipe on page 22.

Materials:

- 1" x 18" strips of muslin
- needles and thread
- scissors
- printed fabric
- 12" x 12" pieces of muslin

Directions:

1. Let each child choose a printed fabric to use for his or her apron. Cut out one 12" x 12" piece of the selected fabric for each child.
2. Lay each piece of fabric on a flat surface with the printed side up. Place a 12" x 12" piece of muslin on top of the fabric.
3. Help each child sew around three sides of the apron.

4. Turn the apron right-side-out. Then complete the square by sewing the fourth side closed.
5. Give each child two 1" x 18" strips of muslin. Help them sew one strip to each side of the top of the apron, as shown.
6. Tie to fit around each student's waist.

Applesauce Recipe

Materials:

- 2 dozen apples
- peeler
- corer
- knives
- medium-sized saucepan
- water
- sugar
- large wooden spoon
- large colander
- mixing bowl
- paper plates and plastic spoons

Directions:

1. Have children wash the apples thoroughly.

2. Peel and core the apples. Help students cut the apples into quarters (or other small pieces).

3. Place the apples in a medium-sized saucepan and cover with water.

4. Cook the apples over medium heat until they are soft.

5. When they are done, add some sugar (to taste) to the apples. Mash and stir the applesauce.

6. Drain the applesauce in a large colander. Place the applesauce into a mixing bowl and serve.

Yield: approximately 20 servings

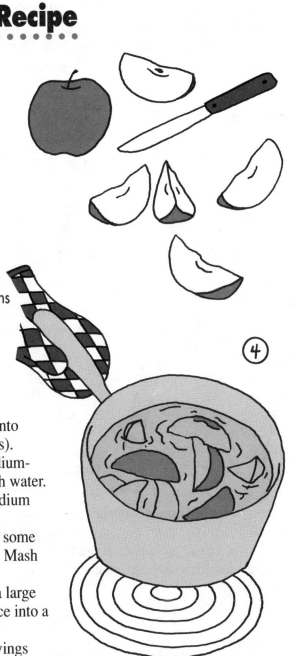

Production Problems

Put the drawings in each row below in the proper order. Write the number 1 in the box that shows the first step in production, the number 2 in the box showing the second step, and so on.

Color the pictures. Then try to draw a production sequence of your own!

Model Neighborhood

Materials:

- large plywood board
- empty boxes and cartons of all sizes and shapes
- aluminum foil (optional)
- fabric scraps (optional)
- jar lids of all sizes
- pipe cleaners
- crayons and markers
- scissors
- construction paper
- old magazines
- clothespins
- collage materials
- glue

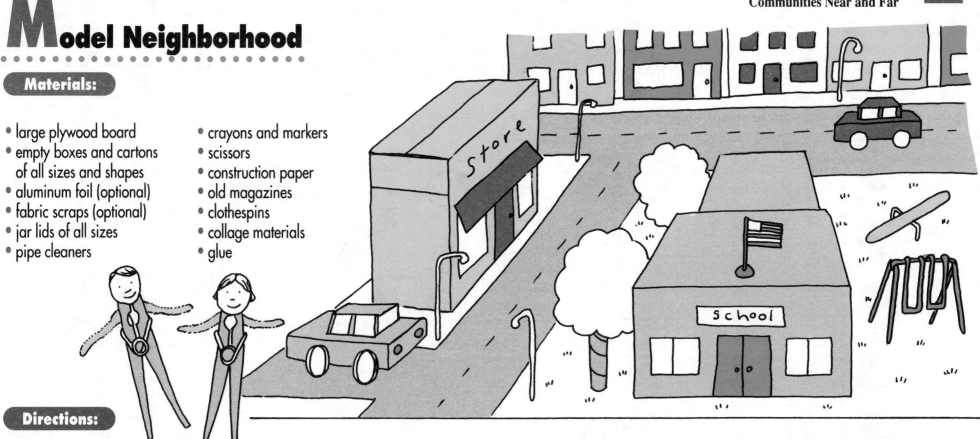

Directions:

1. Take a walking tour of the block around the school. Note the types of buildings and whether they are commercial or residential, what type of landscaping there is, whether there are parks or roadways, and what different types of people frequent the area.

2. Have the class create buildings they saw on their tour from empty cardboard boxes and cartons. Select them for proper size and shape, then cover them in the appropriate color of construction paper. If desired, add aluminum-foil windows and use fabric scraps for curtains.

3. Lay the buildings out in the correct sequence on a board base. Cut construction paper roads and glue them to the base.

4. Create street lights, telephone and electrical lines, and railings, using pipe cleaners. Use jar lids for wheels on vehicles.

5. Cut people's faces from old magazines and glue them onto the tops of clothespins. Add pipe-cleaner arms and use the open end as legs. Glue the people to benches, outside of stores, and in yards doing lawn work or talking to neighbors.

6. Review the model with the class. Have they included enough parks and playgrounds? Are the nearby buildings all shown? Make any adjustments according to students' comments.

7. After the model is completed to the class's satisfaction, display it to other classes. Ask them to identify some buildings that are in the neighborhood. If possible, take a picture of the model with the class behind it and attach it to the base.

List of Errands File Folder Game

Materials:

- crayons or markers
- scissors
- letter-sized file folder
- glue
- clear contact paper
- envelope
- die

Directions:

1. Reproduce the "How to Play" directions, the game board on pages 26 and 27, and the playing pieces on page 28 once each. Reproduce the errand game cards on page 28 four times. Color and cut everything out.

2. Glue the "How to Play" directions to the front of a file folder.

3. Glue the game board to the inside of the file folder, with inner edges touching as shown.

4. Laminate the playing pieces and game cards.

5. Glue an envelope to the back of the file folder for storage of game cards and playing pieces.

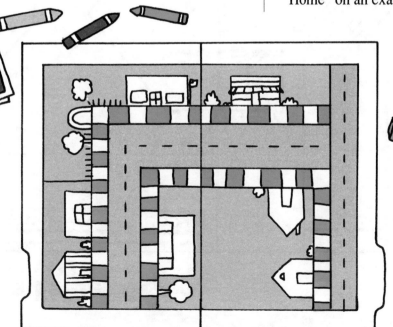

How to Play
(for 2 to 4 players)

1. Place all the playing pieces on "Home." Shuffle the game cards and place them in a pile alongside the game board. The oldest player goes first, and play continues clockwise around the game board.

2. Have each player pick six errand cards from the game card pile and lay them out faceup in front of him- or herself.

3. The first player then rolls the die and moves that number of spaces on the sidewalk. A player may cross a street only in the walks provided. Crosswalks count as one space.

4. To complete an errand, a player must roll the exact number of spaces needed to get inside the building or park. When an errand has been "completed," a player may turn the corresponding errand card facedown.

5. The first player to complete all his or her errands and land back on "Home" on an exact count is the winner.

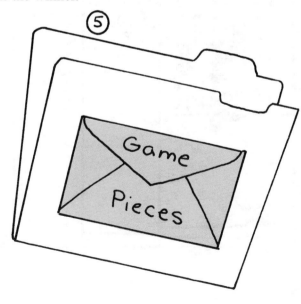

List of Errands File Folder Game

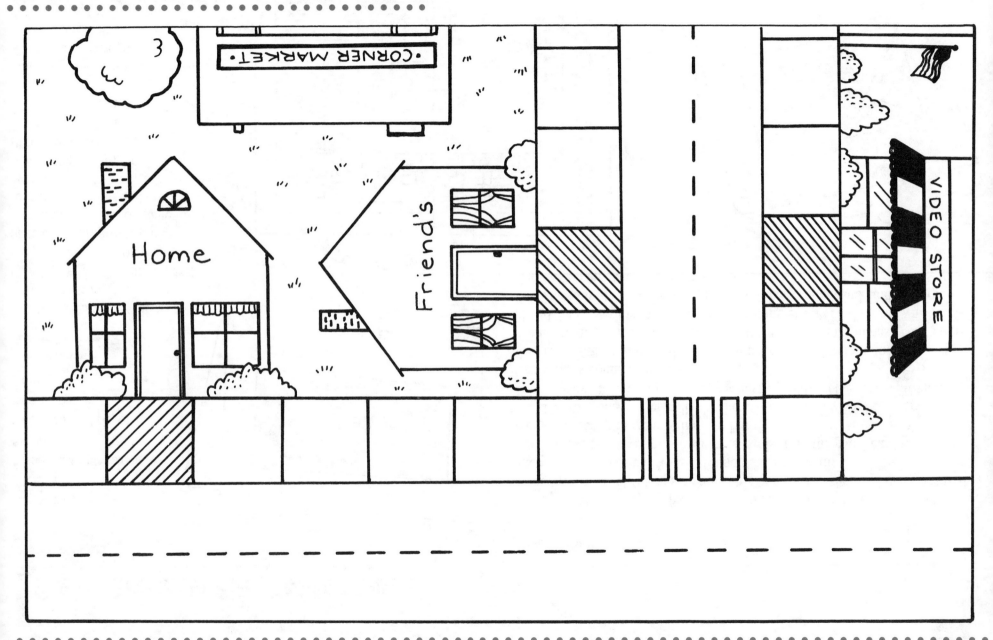

List of Errands File Folder Game

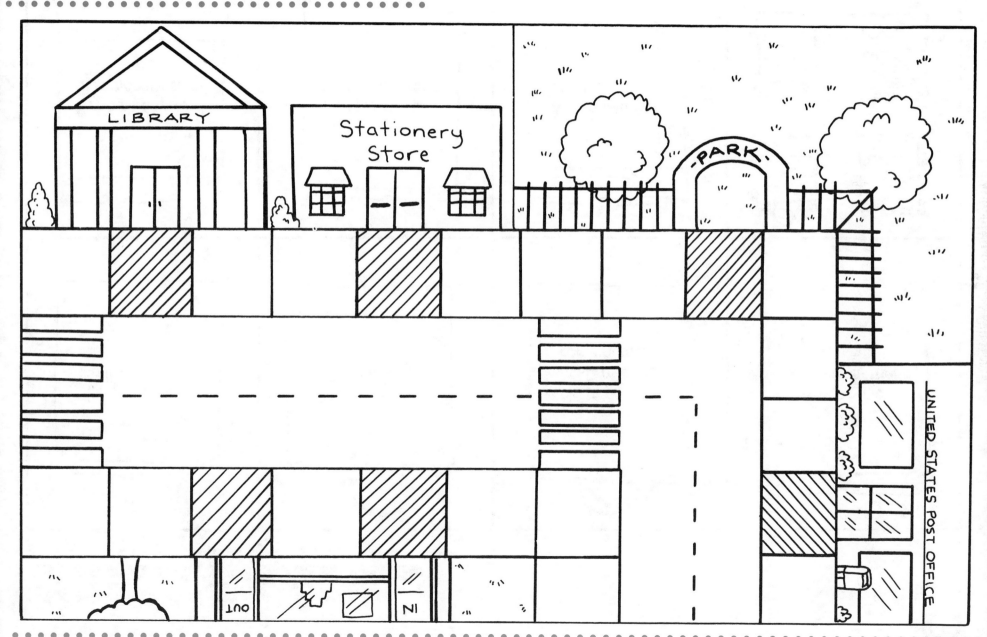

List of Errands File Folder Game

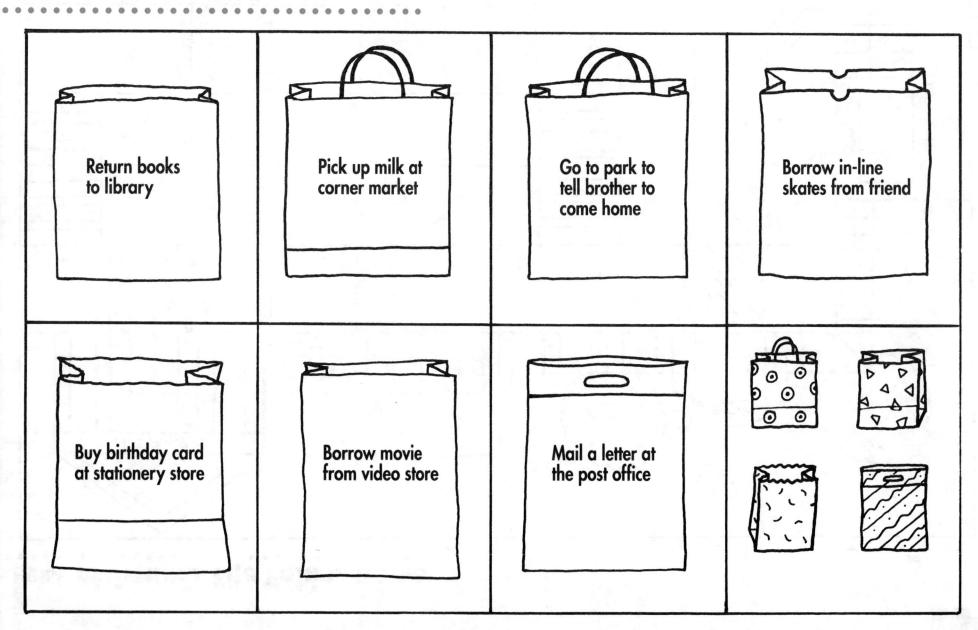

Return books to library

Pick up milk at corner market

Go to park to tell brother to come home

Borrow in-line skates from friend

Buy birthday card at stationery store

Borrow movie from video store

Mail a letter at the post office

Best Books About Communities

Read some or all of the following books to the class during a study unit about their community. Place the books in the class library or reading center for students to look at during free time.

All About Things People Do by Melanie and Chris Rice (Doubleday, 1990)

City/Country by Ken Robbins (Viking, 1985)

Everybody Cooks Rice by Norah Dooley (Carolrhoda, 1991)

Friendship Across Arctic Waters: Alaskan Cub Scouts Visit Their Soviet Neighbors by Claire Rudolf Murphy (Lodestar, 1991)

Island Boy by Barbara Cooney (Puffin, 1991)

Night on Neighborhood Street by Eloise Greenfield (Dial, 1991)

This Is a House by Colleen Stanley Bare (Cobblehill, 1992)

When I Was Young in the Mountains by Cynthia Rylant (Dutton, 1982)

Sign Language

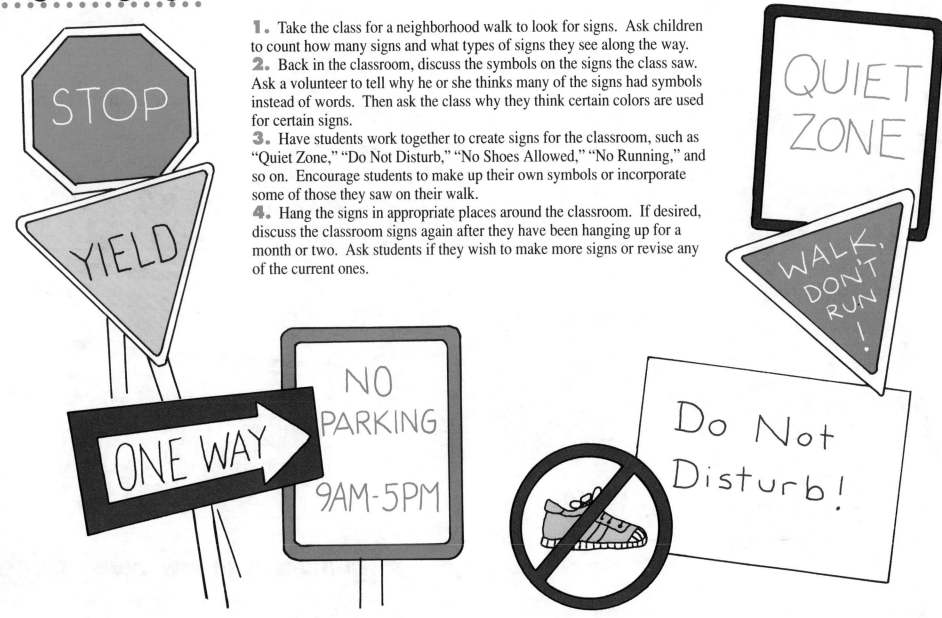

1. Take the class for a neighborhood walk to look for signs. Ask children to count how many signs and what types of signs they see along the way.

2. Back in the classroom, discuss the symbols on the signs the class saw. Ask a volunteer to tell why he or she thinks many of the signs had symbols instead of words. Then ask the class why they think certain colors are used for certain signs.

3. Have students work together to create signs for the classroom, such as "Quiet Zone," "Do Not Disturb," "No Shoes Allowed," "No Running," and so on. Encourage students to make up their own symbols or incorporate some of those they saw on their walk.

4. Hang the signs in appropriate places around the classroom. If desired, discuss the classroom signs again after they have been hanging up for a month or two. Ask students if they wish to make more signs or revise any of the current ones.

Name _____

Take the Train

Look at the train ticket prices at the ticket window. Then answer the questions below.

One-way Fares

New York City to Orlando	**$175**
Washington, D.C., to Atlanta	**$124**
Atlanta to Los Angeles	**$150**
Montreal to Boston	**$96**
St. Louis to Houston	**$124**
Houston to Santa Fe	**$178**
New Orleans to Seattle	**$276**
Omaha to Winnipeg	**$187**
Edmonton to Calgary	**$69**
Phoenix to Boise	**$217**
Detroit to Chicago	**$88**
Chicago to San Francisco	**$249**

TICKET WINDOW

1. You have $100 in your pocket. Name all the possible routes you could take for that

amount. _____

2. If you had $47 and you needed to take a trip from Montreal to Boston, how much

would you have to borrow? _____

3. How much would a round trip from Omaha to Winnipeg cost? _____

4. You begin your trip with $78 and have $9 left over to buy souvenirs. Which route

did you take? _____

5. How much would it cost to travel from St. Louis to Santa Fe? _____

6. Which routes have prices with a seven in the tens place? _____

_____

7. How much would it cost to travel from Detroit to San Francisco? _____

How much would the round trip be? _____

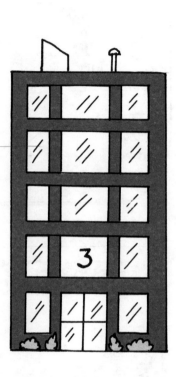

Neighborhood Numbers

Materials:

- crayons or markers
- scissors
- oaktag
- glue
- clear contact paper

Directions:

1. Reproduce the house pictures on page 33 several times. Ask students to color the pictures, mount them on oaktag, and cut them out.

2. Laminate the pictures with clear contact paper.

3. Play several math games using the pictures. Some suggestions are:

Numerical Order—Write a number on each house. Then have the class line them up in numerical order.

Ordinal Numbers—Ask the class to put the houses in order using ordinal numbers (for example, "Put the red house first, the green house second, the trailer third," and so on). Or place the homes in a line and ask students to

use ordinal numbers to identify which house you are describing (for example "Where on the line is the apartment building?").

Spatial Directions—Ask students to move the houses according to directions, such as "Put the red house below the green house" or "Move the blue house so it is between the pink and the purple ones."

More/Less—Place some houses close together on one side of the table and the same number more loosely scattered on the other side. Ask which side has more houses. Repeat, using a different number of houses. Then ask which side has fewer houses.

Neighborhood Numbers

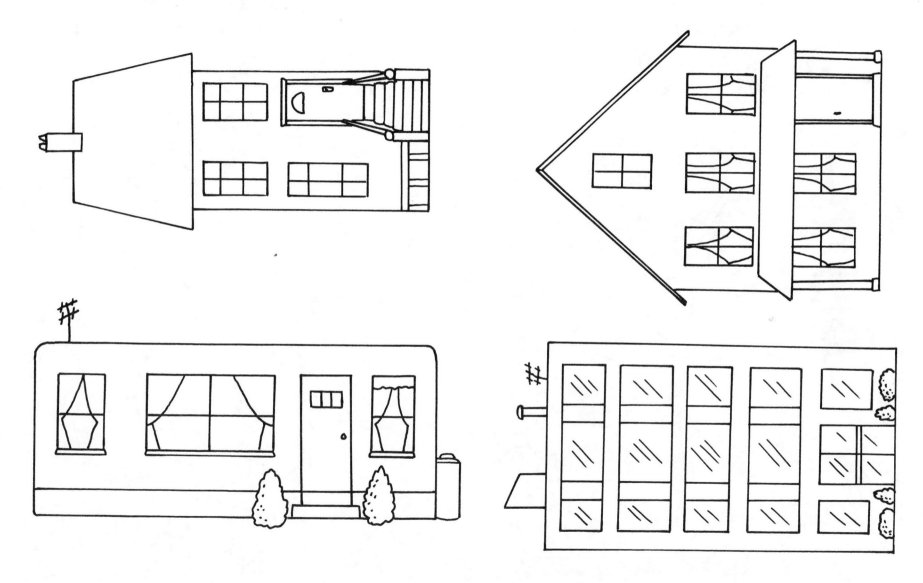

Name _____

At the Park

Circle all the things that do not belong in the park.

Supermarket ABCs

1. Arrange a field trip to a local supermarket. Help students notice the workers and what their jobs are, the various sections of the market and how the items are sorted, the variety of products, the machines used, and deliveries to the store.

2. After visiting the supermarket, ask children to bring in clean, empty cans, containers, boxes, and cartons from home.

3. Create a minisupermarket in the classroom. Some suggested activities are:

• Have the students stock the shelves according to a sorting system. For example, have them place all red items or all items beginning with a certain letter on one shelf, or sort according to use of the product, or sort by whether the item is a fruit, vegetable, or grain.

• Alphabetize the products according to the first letter on the label.

• Have children write stories using the names of the foods.

• Match products having the same names or the same beginning, medial, or ending sounds.

Do more/less comparisons. Find all the *o*'s on a box and count them. Find all the *th*'s on a container and count them. Are there more on one box than on another?

Show sequencing pictures of how a product gets to market.

Compare and contrast children's items with adults' items. How is the packaging different?

Compare and contrast prices of generic products with prices of brand-name products.

Name _____

Shapes in Architecture

Take a walk around a block in your neighborhood. As you walk, place a check in the appropriate column each time you see one of the shapes below used in a building.

Write the total for each column on the lines provided at the bottom of the chart.

■	●	▬	◆	▲	⬤

Total: _____ _____ _____ _____ _____ _____

Now create a building using all the shapes pictured above.

Transportation Concentration Game

- crayons or markers
- scissors
- oaktag
- glue
- clear contact paper

Directions:

1. Reproduce the game cards on pages 38 and 39 twice. Color the cards, mount them on oaktag, and cut them out.

2. Laminate the cards. To begin play, shuffle the cards and lay them face-down. For instructions, see "How to Play."

3. For game variations, you may also wish to use the cards to create a "How I Come to School" graph. Glue the pictures along the bottom of a large piece of paper or oaktag. Ask each student to write his or her name on a small rectangle of paper and glue it above the picture that shows how he or she travels to school. Count the totals for each column. Discuss which column totals more, less, the most, the fewest, or equal amounts. Then discuss why students travel to school in different ways.

4. As a transportation extension activity, ask volunteers to describe the different forms of transportation they would use when going to a particular place. Take out a map of the United States and Canada. Ask questions such as, "If you wanted to travel from Florida to Montreal, how might you go?"

5. Discuss travel safety with the class. Ask students to describe how they can keep themselves safe while on a boat, riding a horse, or riding an escalator. Write students' safety suggestions on a large piece of oaktag.

How to Play
(for two players)

1. Spread the cards out facedown on a table.

2. The younger player goes first. That player chooses two cards and turns them faceup. If the cards match, he or she may put them aside and go again. If the cards do not match the cards are turned facedown again and the next player goes.

3. When all the pairs have been matched, each player counts his or her pairs. The player with more pairs win.

Transportation Concentration Game

Transportation Concentration Game

Logic Boxes

Make a mark in each box as you receive information. Using the process of elimination, find the answers to the questions below.

	mountains	river	city
Tina			
Chris			
Terry			

1. Each of the children in the Rios family has a pen pal in a different part of the country: the mountains, by a river, and in a big city. Tina does not write to anyone living by a river. Chris's pen pal does not live in a city. Terry's pen pal does not live in the mountains or by a river. Whose pen pal lives in the mountains, whose lives by a river, and whose lives in a city?

2. Sam, Elise, and Joel all belong to a writer's club. Each person contributes something for each meeting: paper, pencils, or cookies. Sam never brings the paper or cookies. Elise does not bring the pencils. Joel does not bring the paper. Who brings which contribution to the meetings?

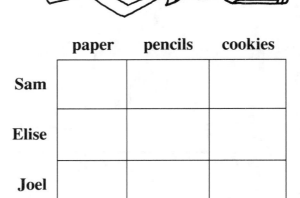

	paper	pencils	cookies
Sam			
Elise			
Joel			

	oldest	youngest	middle
Ted			
Ned			
Ed			

3. Ted, Ned, and Ed are brothers. Ted is not the oldest. Ned is not the youngest. Ed is neither the oldest nor the middle child. Which boy is the oldest, the youngest, and the middle child?

Our Community Game

1 Play a variation of the game "Geography" using the names of local towns, rivers, parks, historic sites, and other places of interest. Gather the class together in a circle.

2. Lead off the game by naming a nearby place with which students are familiar. Then ask the student on your left to take the last letter of the place you have mentioned and use it as the first letter for a new place. For example, if you begin the game with the words "Washington Park," the child on your left would need to come up with a place that begins with the letter *K*.

3. Continue the game around the circle. Encourage students to ask for help if they cannot think of appropriate answers.

4. Play the game for as long as interest holds. Afterwards, ask each child to choose one of the places mentioned in the game and write or dictate a few sentences telling what he or she knows about that place. Have children illustrate the places as well.

5. Hang the pictures on a bulletin board. Title the bulletin board "Places All Around."

6. As an extension activity for older children, ask each student to research the origin of the name of a place he or she has chosen. Encourage students to write down their findings and share the information with the rest of the class.

Community Field Trips

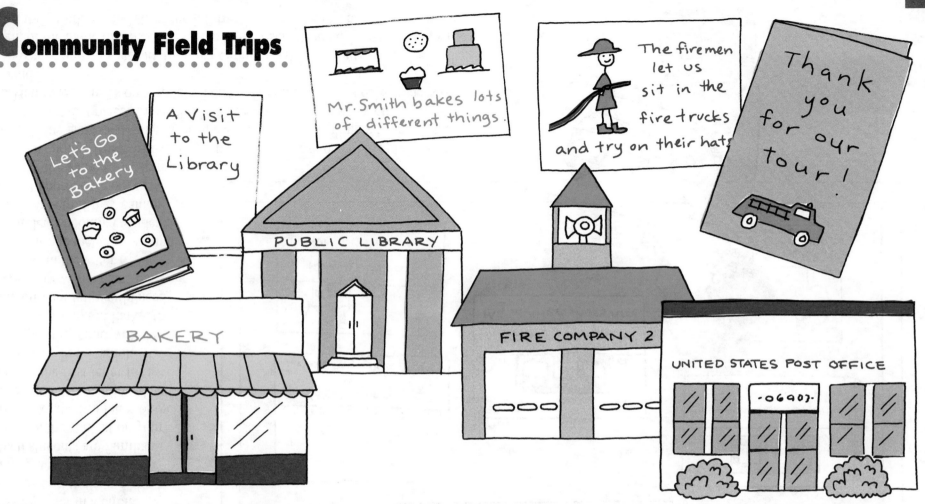

1. Arrange field trips to different community spots, such as a hospital, a doctor's or dentist's office, a senior citizens' home, the post office, the library, a bakery, a restaurant, a park or garden, a fish market, a bank, the fire station, a supermarket, or a pet store.

2. Help students compose questions before each field trip. Encourage children to ask questions beginning "how," "when," "where," "why," and "who " (for example, "Why did you decide to become a dentist?" or "How does all the mail get sorted?").

3. To thank the community workers who volunteered their time, have students create an oversized thank-you card. Children may also wish to participate in an organized cleanup, make decorations for the community workers, or work on fund raisers for the different organizations (if applicable).

4. After each trip, discuss the experience. If possible, find a book, a song, or a poem that reflects the events of each field trip. You may also wish to have students create art projects to bring out the aesthetic side of the trips.

5. Be sure to take photographs or have students draw pictures of what was seen on each trip. Make a graph like that described on page 37 of "My Favorite Trip" with the class and display it near the other post-trip activities.

Classroom Government

1. During a study unit about government, lead a discussion about taxes. Ask volunteers to tell what they know about taxes and why people must pay them.

2. If possible, invite a local elected official or a school board member to discuss how tax money is distributed. (Remind classroom visitors to keep their explanations as simple as possible!)

3. Afterward, have students name some of the ways tax dollars are used (for example, for schools, libraries, road maintenance, police, and fire fighters). Write their comments on an experience chart.

4. Tell students that they will set up their own "taxes" for things used in the classroom. Help students think of ways to use their classroom taxes, such as to buy art supplies, fund field trips, buy snacks, and so on.

5. Let the class vote on their tax decisions. Record the decisions made on a piece of paper. If desired, photocopy the paper once for each child in the class. Let children take the papers home to share their tax decisions with their families.

6. You may also wish to stage an election for class president, using cartoon characters as the candidates. Have students decide what platform each candidate should run on (for example, "More Free Time for First Graders"). Let children work together to create campaign posters and speeches for the different candidates. Then hold a mock election to see which candidate wins!

Classroom Taxes For
- ✓ Art Supplies
- ✓ Fish food
- ✓ Field trips
- ✓ Snacks
- ✓ Story books

VOTE FOR
Jack Rabbit

Dexter Dinosaur
for Class Presi[dent]

Vote

Stone Soup

Once upon a time, there was a man who traveled from town to town. Although he had nothing to his name, this man did possess a natural gift of charm, which often helped him get by.

One day the traveler came to a small village where the people had recently had some hard times. The crops had not been as plentiful as they had been in years past, and everyone was feeling very stingy.

The traveler knocked on the door of the first house he came to. An old man answered.

"I was wondering if I might trouble you for a bite to eat," the traveler said.

"I have nothing to eat myself," said the old man gruffly. "Nobody in this town has any food."

"Nothing to eat!" said the traveler. "Then you must let me help you. I'll make some stone soup. Do you have a big kettle I could borrow?"

The old man thought for a minute. "I might be able to find a kettle," he said. "But what is stone soup?"

The traveler smiled. "It's the best soup in the world," he said. Then he held up a small, smooth stone. "And it's made with this very stone."

The old man was doubtful, but nevertheless he went inside and returned with a huge kettle.

The traveler set the kettle up in the middle of town. He placed the stone in the bottom of the kettle and added some water. Then he started a fire under the kettle.

The other townspeople came out to watch. The old man explained to them what the traveler was making.

The traveler smiled happily. "Just wait until you taste this soup," he said. "And you're all welcome to have some. Of course, it would be even better if we had a few carrots to add."

The townspeople were quiet. Then one woman said, "I might have a few carrots." She ran home and quickly returned with a huge armful of carrots.

The traveler mixed the carrots in. "Wonderful!" he said. "This stone soup will taste great! Now if we only had a potato or two . . ."

"I've got some potatoes," called a boy from the back of the crowd. He went home and came back with a big basket filled with potatoes.

The traveler added the potatoes to the soup. "Mmmm!" he said, stirring the soup. "I remember one time when I thickened the stone soup with a little flour. Now that was a magnificent soup!"

No sooner had the traveler finished speaking than another woman dashed into her house and brought out a bag of flour.

Before too long, everyone had contributed something to the soup. Celery, beef, green peppers, onions, and other good foods were all mixed in. Finally, the traveler added some salt and pepper and declared the soup ready.

Everyone in town had a generous helping of the soup. As they sat around talking and laughing, all the people had to agree—there's nothing better than a bowl of stone soup!

Stone Soup Puppets

1. During a study unit on sharing and working together, read "Stone Soup" aloud to the class. Then reproduce the drawings below and on page 46 once.
2. Color the drawings, mount them on oaktag, and cut them out. Cut along the dash lines on the kettle. Staple a 1" x 3" oaktag strip around the back of each figure to fit around a child's hand.
3. Let students use the puppets and props to act out the story of "Stone Soup."

Stone Soup Puppets

Flour

Worldwide Travelers

1. Ask each student to plan a trip to another country to see how families there live. Provide children with a list of places that have different cultures and ways of living.

2. After each student has chosen or been assigned a country, help him or her research the country. Tell children that they will need to find out about family life, school, work, play, chores, holidays, and other important things. Give students a list of questions to answer, such as:

How does this community differ from your own?
Are the roles for men and women different from their roles in your own country?
What kinds of schools do the children attend?
What family responsibilities do the children have?
What kinds of games and hobbies do the children like to participate in?

3. After students have gathered information about their countries, ask them to draw pictures that illustrate life in their countries. Help each child write a sentence or two that tells about each illustration.

4. Have each student gather his or her illustrations and comments together in an order to make a presentation.

5. Let students present their research to the rest of the class, or divide the class into small groups and have children show their work to the other members of their group.

6. As an extension activity, ask each child to figure out how he or she might travel to his or her chosen country. Is there more than one way to get there? How much would it cost?

Great Britain

Most children in London live in row houses.

Children wear uniforms to school.

They play a game called cricket.

What a Family Means

1. Have a class discussion about different kinds of families in the local community or in other communities near and far. Ask volunteers to name some types of families they have seen or heard about. Write down the make-up of these families on an experience chart.

2. Ask students to tell what makes families different from each other. What qualities do most families have in common? What do families depend on each other for? Encourage students to realize that despite surface differences, people are very much alike all over the world.

3. Have students name some qualities that describe a family. Write these words on another experience chart.

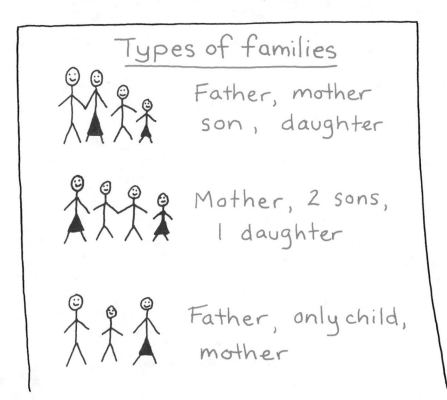

4. Distribute writing paper to the class. Ask each student to write one or two sentences about each of his or her close family members. Tell children to begin their sentences with, "My grandmother (substitute appropriate family member) is . . ." Have students describe what they think the characteristics of this family member are. (Children may wish to refer to the words on the experience chart). For example, a student may write, "My grandmother is a person who works hard at her job, likes to go to baseball games, and reads funny stories to her grandchildren at night."

5. Let children write descriptions for as many family members as they wish. When everyone has completed his or her descriptions, have students punch holes along the left sides of their papers, then tie them together to make a book. If desired, let students make covers and think of titles for their books.

Dream House

1. Explain to students what blueprint plans are. Try to obtain some blueprints from a home design magazine to show children how a blueprint represents the rooms and dimensions of a house. (If possible, invite an architect or builder to the classroom to show some plans and discuss the different aspects of building a house.)

2. Tell students that they will be designing their own one-story homes. Distribute sheets of graph paper to each student. Let children tape two or four sheets together to make a larger "blueprint."

3. Have each student pencil in a basic outline for his or her house. Tell children to show first where they wish the front door to be.

4. After discussing the concept of scale with children, ask students to continue designing the interiors of their homes. Make sure children include the number of bedrooms and bathrooms they wish, a kitchen and dining room, a living room, and any other rooms they would like.

5. Tell students to remember to indicate closets, doors, and windows.

6. Have children draw pictures of what their homes would look like from the outside.

7. When all the "blueprints" are completed, hang them on a classroom wall or a bulletin board with the accompanying illustrations under the title "Our Dream Homes."

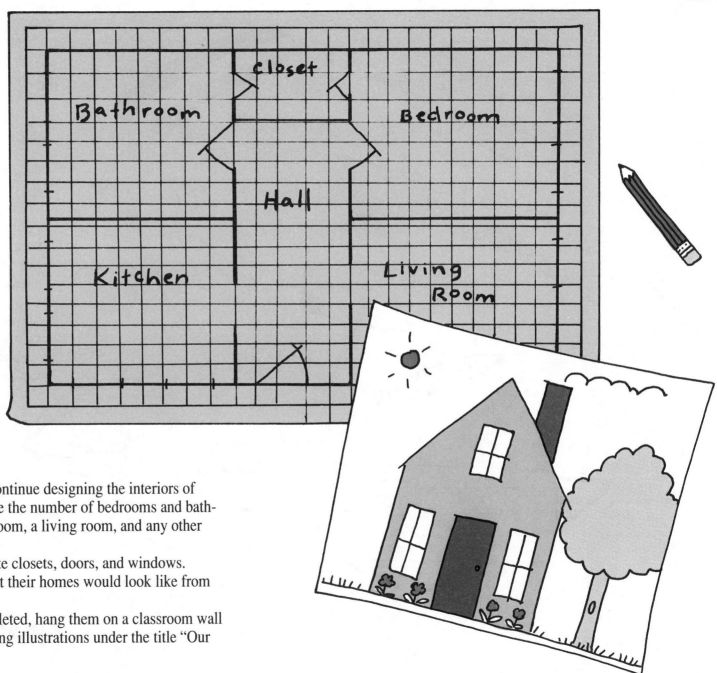

"Time For Play" Mobile

Materials:

- crayons or markers
- construction paper
- oaktag
- glue
- collage materials
- pipe cleaners
- fabric scraps
- wire hangers
- yarn
- transparent tape

Directions:

1. Have a discussion with the class about what they like to do after school and on weekends. What types of activities do they do? Where do they go? Whom do they see? Write the answers on a piece of experience chart paper.

2. Make play mobiles with the class. Lay out construction paper, glue, collage materials, and other objects that the students may use to create replicas of their nonschool activities: reading, riding bicycles, doing arts and crafts, writing, watching television, playing video games, visiting museums and other places of interest, going to the park, visiting friends and relatives, talking on the telephone, and so on. Mount the objects on oaktag and cut them out.

3. Help each student hang the selected objects on a hanger, using yarn. Tape each object in place on the hanger.

4. Ask each child to create a banner on oaktag to cover the empty space on the hanger. Suggest titles for the banners, such as "Time For Play!"

Baby Talk

1. After a class discussion about families, invite a parent to come in with a baby to demonstrate child care to the class.

2. Make sure students have washed their hands thoroughly before having any contact with the baby.

3. Ask volunteers to tell what they know about babies. Encourage children who have had experience with babies to talk about what they have learned.

4. After the classroom visit, ask each child to bring in a picture of him- or herself as a baby. Make sure there are no identifying names or objects in the picture. Tell students to write their names on the backs of the pictures.

5. Mount the baby pictures randomly on a bulletin board. Title the board, "Who Am I?" Write a number next to each picture.

6. Ask children to look at the numbered photographs and try privately to guess the name of each classmate shown. Have students write their guesses down on paper, matching names to photograph numbers.

7. After everyone has completed their guesses, tell students the answers. Let each child correct his or her own paper. See if anyone guessed every picture correctly.

8. Ask volunteers to tell why they made the guesses they did. What were some of the similarities and differences between the photographs and the way their classmates look now?

9. Have a class discussion about change. Point out to students that almost everything changes in some way over time—their bodies, families, schools, and so on. Explain that communities also change and need to be changed. Roads, schools, libraries, and other community things need repair and maintenance and to change their character as the community around them changes.

10. Ask volunteers to name some ways they have changed as they have grown older. Write their comments on an experience chart. Title the chart "I'm Changing Every Day."

Fire Safety Bulletin Board

Materials:

- see-through pot with lid
- candle
- matches
- crayons or markers
- scissors
- construction paper
- red bulletin board paper
- stapler

Directions:

1. Ask each child in the class to turn to someone sitting next to him or her. Have each student tell that person all the fire safety rules the student knows (for example, "Call the fire department immediately in case of a fire"). Then have each listener tell the class one thing the other student told them.

2. Display books about firefighters and fire safety. Read and discuss several books with the class.

3. Perform a fire safety experiment. Place a candle in a see-through pot. Light the candle and put the lid on top to seal the pot.

4. Ask students to predict what might happen to the flame. (In a few minutes, the light should go out.) Explain to the class that the fire has consumed all the oxygen in the pot. Without oxygen, the fire will die out.

5. Have a volunteer demonstrate "Stop, Drop, and Roll," a technique to be used if one's clothing catches on fire. Tell students that by rolling and laying on the fire, they can block oxygen from getting to it. This will extinguish the fire. Ask all students to practice this drill.

6. As a homework assignment as well as an ongoing lesson, make sure students know their full names, their parents' names, their home addresses, and their telephone numbers.

7. If your community uses the "Dial 911" emergency system, practice calling 911 on a toy telephone with the class. Stress that children should always practice using a toy—only in an emergency are they to use a real phone and dial 911. Inform students that the emergency workers at 911 will ask them what the problem is as well as the location of the emergency. Have them pretend to give the necessary information. If possible, ask a 911 worker to come to the classroom to demonstrate how various emergencies are handled.

8. Plan a field trip to a local fire station. Make a list of questions the class would like to ask the firefighters. Take a camera along to photograph the trucks, uniforms, and special equipment firefighters use.

9. On returning to the classroom, create a bulletin board about fire safety with the class. Decorate the background with red paper. Ask students to draw pictures about something they think is important for others to know about the topic. Have students dictate or write messages on their illustrations. Then staple the pictures to the board. Title the bulletin board, "What You Know Could Save Lives."

Safety First Bulletin Board

1. Invite a police officer into the classroom to talk to the class about safety. Before the officer arrives, encourage students to think up questions they would like answered about being a police officer. Some suggested questions are:

Why do police officers wear uniforms?
What are the things in your belt called and what do they do?
What are some of the things you do every day?
What is the best thing about your job?
Why did you decide to become a police officer?
What is the most dangerous part of your job?

2. Ask the officer to explain the purpose of 911 (if appropriate) and why it is important for students to know their full names, their parents' names, and their addresses and telephone numbers.

3. If possible, arrange a field trip to a police station. Bring along a camera to take pictures of students at various parts of the station.

4. Back in the classroom, have students draw pictures of the things that they noticed most at the station. Ask each student to write on the paper or dictate a few sentences about the visit.

5. Have the class compose a thank-you note to the officers who spoke with them. Include several photographs and student illustrations if possible.

I liked the sirens and the lights

Thank you Officer Thurston for our tour of the police station. We learned a lot.

Milk Carton Bird Feeder

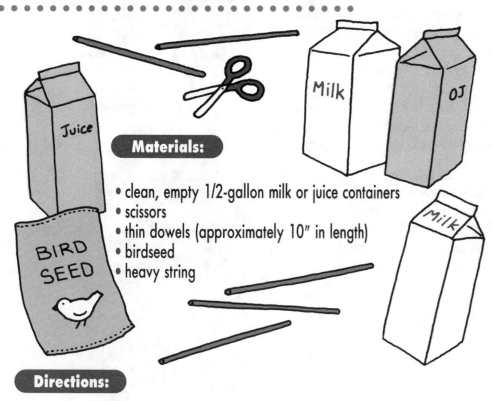

Materials:

- clean, empty 1/2-gallon milk or juice containers
- scissors
- thin dowels (approximately 10" in length)
- birdseed
- heavy string

Directions:

1. Ask each child to bring in a clean, empty half-gallon milk or juice container from home.

2. Help students cut out two sides of the container, leaving 1" of container around the bottom of the cutout sides, as shown.

3. Show children how to use a pencil to make two holes for a thin 10" dowel to go through across the bottom.

4. Push a dowel through the holes to make a perch for the feeder.

5. Punch a hole near the top of each bird feeder. Loop a short length of heavy string through the hole and tie to make a hanger.

6. Have students place birdseed inside each feeder. Let children hang the bird feeders outside the classroom or take them home to hang in their yards.

Recycling Rights and Wrongs

Circle each picture below that shows something that can be recycled. Put an "X" on each picture showing something that cannot be recycled.

Environmental Word Search

Create your own word search puzzle using the words in the box below. Remember, the words may appear forward, backward, up, down, or diagonally.

| recycle | plastic | paper | water | chemical |
| ecology | environment | earth | air | pollution |

When you're finished, give your puzzle to a friend or family member to solve!

Our Weather

Fill in the dates and any holiday names for this month on the calendar below. Each day, draw a picture of what the weather is like.

Sun	Mon	Tues	Wed	Thurs	Fri	Sat

Animal Families

Animals have families, too! Draw lines to connect each family pair. (One has been done for you.)

The Mitten

One cold winter's day, a little boy was sent out into the woods to bring back some firewood. After the boy had loaded up his wheelbarrow with sticks and logs, he headed for home. But just as he grabbed hold of the wheelbarrow, one of his mittens slipped off and fell in the snow.

Now, the boy was cold and tired and wanted to rush home as quickly as he could. So he left his mitten where it lay and hurriedly pushed the wheelbarrow through the woods and back to his house.

Just as soon as the boy left, a little mouse spotted the mitten. Since the mouse was very cold and the mitten looked very warm, he decided to snuggle up inside.

"This is just the right size," the mouse said contentedly.

But before too long a big frog came hopping by. The frog also was chilled in the cold snow.

"May I come in?" she called to the mouse. "It's so very cold out here."

"All right," said the tiny mouse. "But hurry in before it gets too chilly in here."

"This is just the right size for us," the frog said happily as she snuggled in with the mouse.

No sooner had she said that than a blue jay swooped down.

"Hello in there!" he called. "May I please join you?"

"All right!" said the mouse and the frog. "Hurry in!"

The bird quickly flew into the mitten. "It's lovely in here," he said. "And just the right size for the three of us!"

Just then a rabbit bounded up to the mitten. "M-m-m-may I-I-I-I c-c-c-come in?" she asked, her teeth chattering.

"All right!" everyone answered. "But hurry!"

The rabbit had to squish and turn to fit inside the mitten. "There!" she said when she was finally settled. "This mitten is just the right size for us all!"

Suddenly a long snout came into the mitten. "Hi!" said a red fox. "I couldn't help but notice that you all looked mighty warm in there. May I please join you?"

"All right!" they all called.

They did not bother to tell the fox to hurry, because they knew it would take quite a bit of effort for him to fit inside the mitten. But sure enough, he did.

"Ahhhh!" he said. "I'm nice and warm now, too. This mitten is just the right size for us all!"

But who should appear at that moment but a huge, cold bear! "Please help me," he said. "I'm freezing!"

"There's no more room!" squeaked the mouse.

"We can't fit anyone else in here!" added the frog.

"Let's see about that," said the bear. And he proceeded to twist and turn and paw his way into the mitten.

First one seam popped. Then another, and another, and another. Soon everyone was out in the cold snow, and the little mitten was ripped to pieces.

"Now look what you've done!" said the mouse. "We'll all freeze to death!"

"I'm sorry," said the bear. "But perhaps we can all help each other." Then he had an idea.

The bear told the others his plan. In just a few minutes, the new friends snuggled up together in a cozy little group, warming each other.

"I've never been so warm," sighed the happy mouse. "And best of all, this is exactly the right size for us all!"

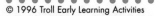

The Mitten Flannel Board

During a study unit on cooperation, read "The Mitten" aloud to the class. First reproduce the figures on this page and page 61 once. Color the figures and cut them out. Then place scraps of flannel or sandpaper on the back of each figure. Move the figures around the flannel board as you read "The Mitten."

The Mitten Flannel Board

Outstanding Service Award

(name)

(service performed)

(presented by)

(date)

Community Service Award

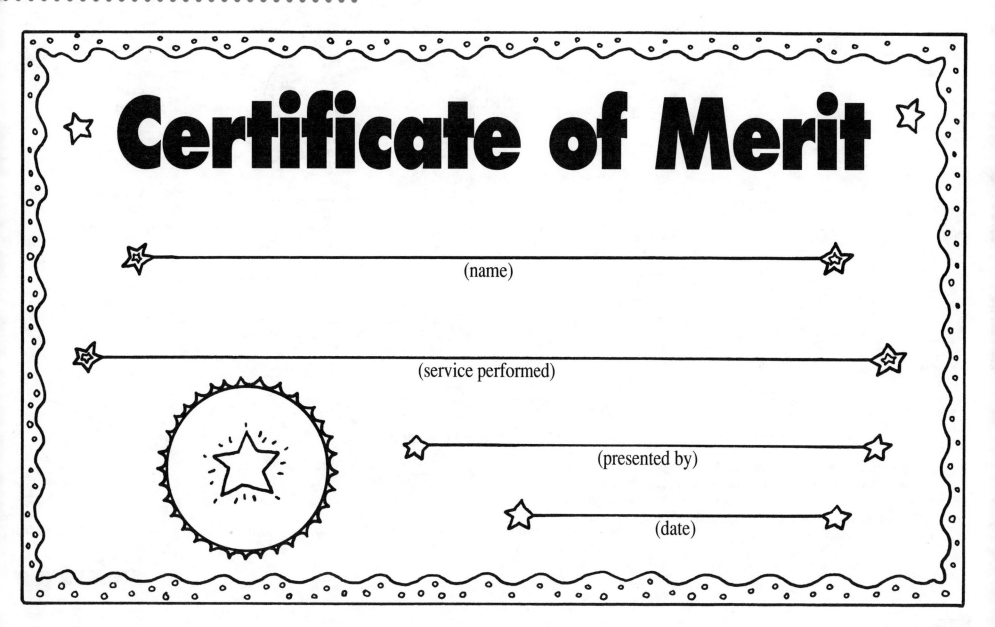

Certificate of Merit

_____ (name)

_____ (service performed)

_____ (presented by)

_____ (date)

Answers

page 20

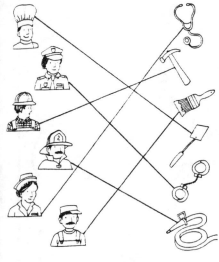

page 23

page 31

1. Montreal to Boston;
   Edmonton to Calgary;
   Detroit to Chicago
2. $49
3. $374
4. Edmontom to Calgary
5. $302
6. New York City to Orlando;
   Houston to Santa Fe;
   New Orleans to Seattle
7. $337; $674

page 34

page 40

1. Tina's pen pal lives in the mountains, Chris's pen pal lives by a river, and Terry's pen pal lives in a city.
2. Sam brings pencils, Elise brings paper, and Joel brings cookies.
3. Ted is the middle child, Ned is the oldest, and Ed is the youngest.

page 55

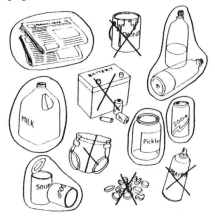

page 58

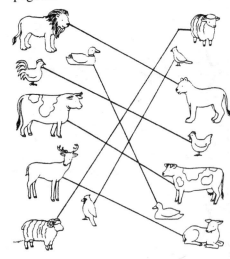

page 56

Answers will vary.

Metric Conversion Chart

1 inch = 2.54 centimeters	1 fluid ounce (oz.) = 29.573 milliliters
1 foot = .305 meter	1 cup = .24 liter
1 yard = .914 meter	1 pint = .473 liter
1 mile = 1.61 kilometers	1 teaspoon = 4.93 milliliters

© 1996 Troll Early Learning Activities